When Frank Was Four

Alison Lester

A LITTLE ARK BOOK

ALLEN & UNWIN

One

When Nicky was one she tipped spaghetti on her head.

Frank bit the dog.

Tessa took her first steps.

Celeste ate the cat food.

Ernie bashed the saucepans.

And Rosie said 'Horse'.

But Clive smashed the china
at his Great Grandmother's birthday party.

Two

When Frank was two he loved to wave goodnight to the moon.

A kangaroo stole Rosie's chips.

Tessa stopped wearing nappies.

Ernie climbed into the fish tank.

Celeste began to sleep all night.

And once at the supermarket, Clive just couldn't wait.

But Nicky got lost on Christmas Eve.

Three

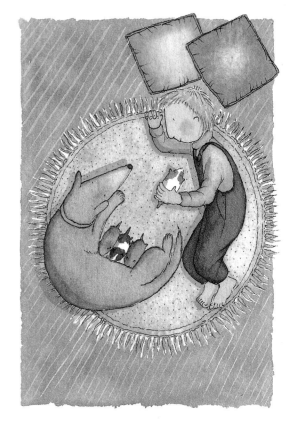

When Clive was three
he danced in his
cousin's tutu.

Ernie gave away his
dummy.

Frank's dog had
puppies.

Rosie began to play the guitar.

Celeste was given a chicken for her birthday.

And Nicky got stuck up a tree.

But Tessa made a pudding.

Four

When Frank was four he ate three packets of fruity fish.

Nicky cut off her plait.

Tessa dressed up the cat.

Ernie started to wear glasses.

Clive took off his training wheels.

And Rosie's pony arrived on Christmas morning.

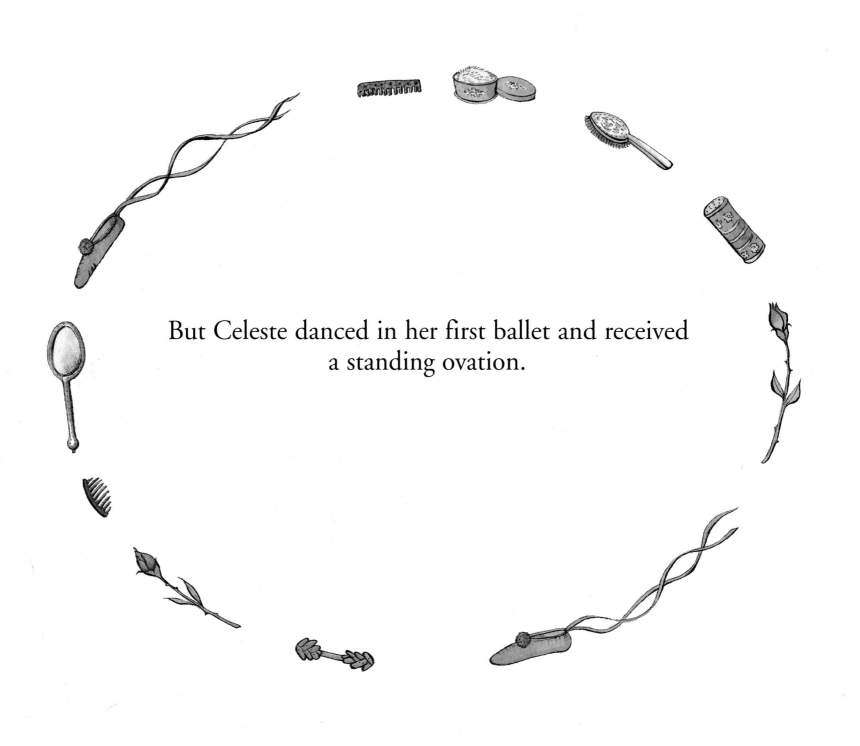

But Celeste danced in her first ballet and received
a standing ovation.

 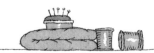

Five

When Ernie was five
he was sure a monster
lived in his cupboard.

Celeste made a
snowman.

Rosie got a baby sister.

Nicky broke her arm.

Clive's mother sewed his alligator duvet.

And Tessa swam right across the pool.

But Frank parachuted off the garage roof.

Six

When Nicky was six she did a somersault on the trampoline.

Frank kidnapped his Grandmother's cat.

Ernie's lizard had babies.

Clive made a
crocodile-shaped
birthday cake.

Tessa ran away from
home.

And Celeste wore her
pyjama pants to
school.

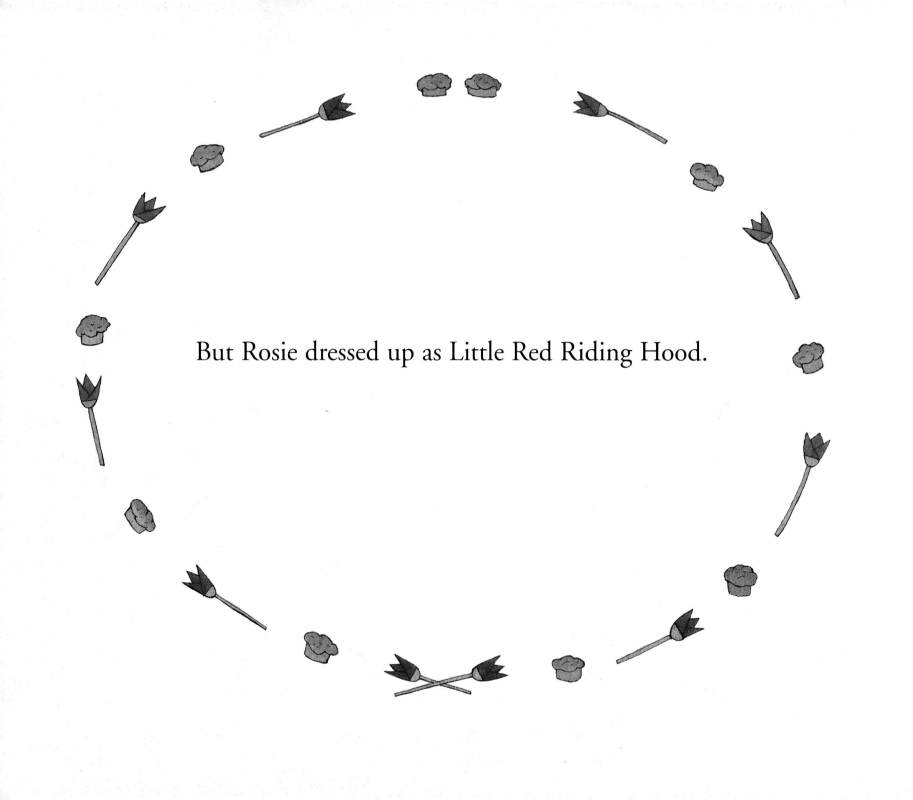

But Rosie dressed up as Little Red Riding Hood.

Seven

When Celeste was seven she had her first filling.

Nicky flew off the swing.

Rosie climbed Uluru.

Frank built a spaceship.

And Tessa gave Clive his first kiss.

But Ernie made a midnight friend.

Clive has	1 alligator duvet	2 goldfish	3 mixing bowls
Nicky has	1 rag doll	2 bouncing balls	3 hammers
Tessa has	1 calico cat	2 bunny slippers	3 wooden spoons
Celeste has	1 rooster	2 tutus	3 birthday balloons
Frank has	1 dog	2 rockets	3 packets of sweets
Rosie has	1 cowgirl hat	2 riding boots	3 show ribbons
Ernie has	1 dummy	2 saucepan lids	3 dinosaurs

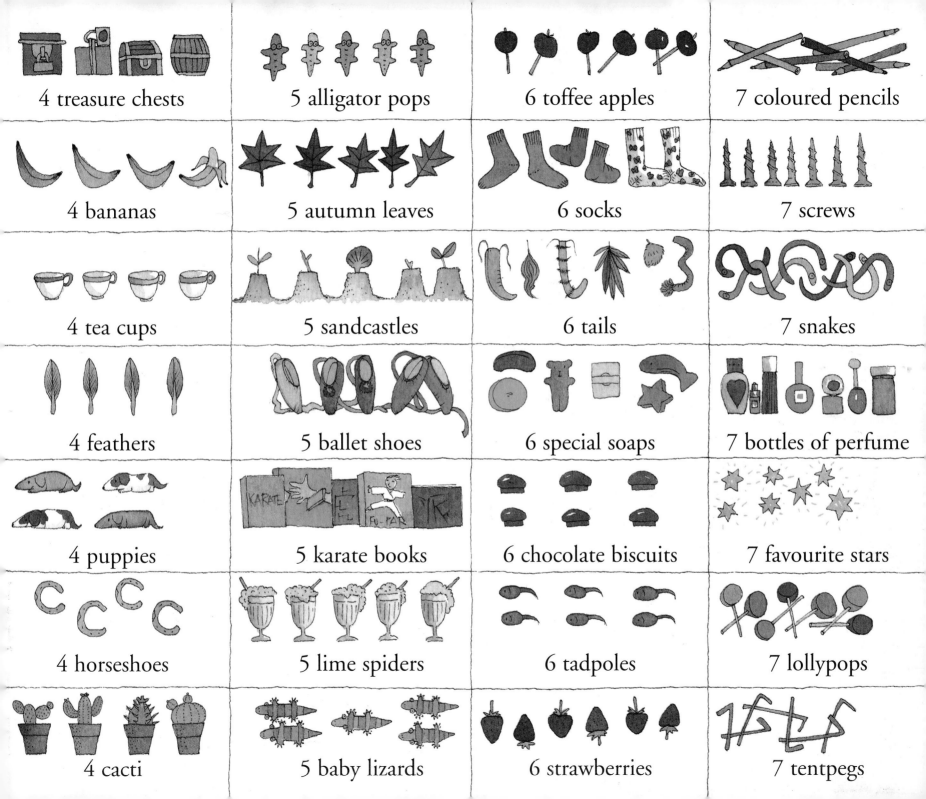

4 treasure chests	5 alligator pops	6 toffee apples	7 coloured pencils
4 bananas	5 autumn leaves	6 socks	7 screws
4 tea cups	5 sandcastles	6 tails	7 snakes
4 feathers	5 ballet shoes	6 special soaps	7 bottles of perfume
4 puppies	5 karate books	6 chocolate biscuits	7 favourite stars
4 horseshoes	5 lime spiders	6 tadpoles	7 lollypops
4 cacti	5 baby lizards	6 strawberries	7 tentpegs

Ourselves

For Helen and Woofa

A Little Ark Book
First published in the UK in 1997
by Allen & Unwin UK Ltd
Studio 6, 123 Liverpool Road
Islington, London N1 1LA
Phone & Fax: (44 171) 607 5050
First published in Australia in 1994
by Hodder Headline Australia Pty Ltd

ISBN 1 86448 399 7
ISBN 1 86448 400 4 (pb)

Produced by Mandarin Offset